Crystal Grids

*A Guide to Using Crystal Grids
for Healing and Manifestation*

Taylor Turner

Table of Contents

Introduction

Are you ever amazed at how the earth offers the most stunning, naturally beautiful gifts? Coveted jewels and precious metals are developed in the very ground we walk upon. When you hold a crystal and gaze into its mystical layers and shimmering depths, it's easy to believe that such a captivating object is powerful. The crystal you hold in your hand could be hundreds, thousands, even millions of years old, created by forces older than time, like volcanos and meteorites. It's no wonder that these incredible stones, each one so unique, have fascinated people since the earliest civilizations.

While crystals may seem like a current trend, they've been revered since ancient times. Gems that can be easily obtained from online metaphysical shops, like carnelian and amethyst, have been found in ancient Egyptian tombs. Octavius Caesar was rumored to be so in love with a single opal that he offered to give up a third of his vast Roman empire just to have it for his crown. Greek warriors covered their bodies with powdered hematite to protect them in battle.

For thousands of years, gemstones have been used in elixirs, ground into medicine, and fashioned into weapons. They've also been worn to attract love, carried to bring prosperity, and placed in the home for serenity. Most of all, they have been considered to have the ability to interact with your physical and energy bodies to bring healing of all kinds. These beliefs are still thriving today.

Alongside the crystal trend, you may have noticed some esoteric-looking geometric designs. Again, these aren't just a fad for clothing and housewares; these ancient symbols are part of what's known as sacred geometry, and when combined with the power of crystals, can do amazing things. Sacred geometry is the shapes and mathematical patterns that weave the very fabric of the entire universe. The spiral of a snail shell mirrors the spiral galaxies in space and even our DNA. The rings of a tree look like the whorls in our fingerprints. Everything in the world and beyond follows the growth patterns of sacred geometry, and with this, we can unite spirituality with science. Aligning with these sacred patterns can help you manifest the life you desire. One way to do this is with crystal grids.

When you put the ancient power of crystals together with the science of sacred geometry in the form of crystal grids, you're creating and harnessing energy in the most powerful way possible.

People often wonder, *can crystal healing really work?* If the last few millennia are any indication, then the answer is yes. Some crystals contain minerals that have therapeutic properties, such as copper. Copper, when worn, can help aching joints and muscles. Some crystals are made into an elixir, which is consumed, allowing the energy of the crystal to work from within the body. Sometimes crystals are applied to an ailing part of the body; the crystal condenses and directs healing energy to the afflicted area. The other benefits of crystal healing are emotional and spiritual. Crystals can be held or placed on the body to release, soften, or ease the mental and emotional body. Because crystals have such an impact on stress levels, they are an excellent tool to include in your mental and emotional health routine. The right crystal, used in the right way, can be a therapeutic, beneficial part of your healing.

Crystals have been scientifically proven to interact with the energy field of other living things. Some crystals intensify energy, while others calm it. When you begin your crystal healing journey, you'll become acquainted with the properties of different stones. As you progress, you will get a feel for how you personally interact with each one.

Crystals are also used for manifestation. This means they can attract various energies and situations into your life like love, prosperity, and peace. Some crystals, when placed on a grid, can impact the entire room or area around them, changing the vibration of a space. Crystal grids can be created for cleansing a room, to open your life to companionship, and to attract happiness into your life. They can be designed to attract energy, like when you're looking to bring love into your life. They can also repel energy for protection. They can even amplify energy to bring strength and vitality.

In this book, you'll learn all about how crystal healing and manifestation work. You'll discover how to select the right crystals for your needs, how to care for them, and what to expect when you begin your journey. We'll discuss the basics of chakra work, one of the most well-known forms of energy healing, and how crystals are an integral part of this practice. From there, you'll learn how and why to cleanse and charge crystals, the ways that shape and color impact their properties, and how to connect with them on an energetic level. You'll also learn all about the sacred geometry in all living things, and how to use crystal grids to enhance your crystal work.

This book includes an alphabetical list of easily obtained crystals, along with their healing properties and metaphysical traits. You'll be able to reference this guide again and again in the future as you work your way along the crystal healing path.

There are examples of crystal grids for a range of intentions that you can try yourself with minimal supplies or experience. With a little practice, you will be able to create your own personalized grids unique to your own specific needs.

Discovering the power of ancient crystals for healing and manifestation will change your life. When done correctly, it can improve your mental and physical health, help clear and focus your mind, and help release emotional blockages that are holding you back.

Crystals and sacred geometry are trending for a reason. People are discovering they're exactly what their body, mind, and spirit need. This timeless phenomenon can be the key to manifesting your best life.

Chapter 1: What Is Crystal Healing?

For those who are new to the concept of crystal healing, it can be difficult to believe that stones can impact a person's wellness, but history shows it's possible. Various kinds of crystal therapies have existed for millennia and are still practiced today. In this chapter, we'll discuss what crystal healing is, how and why it works, and several popular techniques used by healers.

How Do Crystals Work?

Crystals conduct energy, as is seen in many forms of modern technology like radios, computers, and watches. Quartz especially is known to produce energy when compressed, which is called piezoelectricity, and it can even carry an electrical charge. Many kinds of crystals have been scientifically proven to have an electromagnetic field that interacts with our bodies. When you think about how crystals can create and conduct energy like this, it makes sense that they can do the same with healing and spiritual energy. This is the concept that some forms of crystal healing are based on. The compression of a crystal creates a focused stream of energy, so pressing it onto a person's body sends energy into the organ beneath it.

In some practices, the mind, body, and spirit are all connected and equally important. It's believed that physical pain or illness is actually a result of imbalances in the energetic field or emotional issues that have gone unaddressed. In this case, treating the mental, emotional, or spiritual issue can lead to physical healing. You have probably heard the saying that stress manifests in the body, or perhaps you've even experienced it yourself. While stressed you might be more prone to colds, back pain, headaches, and even skin conditions. Stress is a mental and emotional state that impacts the physical system. Western medicine would advise pills and prescription creams, treating only the body. Crystal healing focuses on the stress itself so that physical healing will follow.

When the various bodies—physical, mental, and spiritual—are out of sync, it results in many forms of discomfort or sickness. Crystal therapies aim to balance and align all three of these forms, healing on all levels. When your whole self is integrated into the process, you will be healthier, happier, and better able to live life to its fullest.

To understand how crystal healing works, there are some terminology and concepts to get familiar with. A lot of crystal therapy is based on what are called the chakras, and they're also focused on in a practice called Reiki. Before you begin, it's helpful to be familiar with these concepts and how they work within your body and mind. From there, you can learn about healing and crystal grids, which are based on some of the same concepts as these systems.

Chakras and Crystals

The chakra system originated in India in 1500 B.C.E. and appeared in an ancient text called the Vedas.

In Sanskrit, the word *chakra* means "wheel" or "disk." There are seven major chakras, or energy points, on the human body that are constantly spinning in a clockwise motion. It is believed that the chakras need to be open, healthy, and bright to experience physical, mental, and spiritual wellness. When a chakra is blocked or sluggish, physical and mental symptoms related to that particular chakra may appear as a result.

Each chakra has a color and Sanskrit name, and is linked to a major organ or physical function. Each one also governs a range of emotional and spiritual issues. In crystal healing, each chakra resonates best with a specific crystal. Below are the seven chakras and their associations.

- **Root Chakra (Muladhara).** The root chakra is located at the base of the spine and governs survival, consumption, and elimination. This chakra is associated with your sense of stability in the world, connection to nature, and sense of belonging. Its color is red, and crystals that align best with it are red jasper, hematite, and garnet.

- **Sacral Chakra (Svadhisthana).** The sacral chakra is located just below the navel, and governs the reproductive system. It's associated with emotions, relationships, and creativity. Its color is orange, and some crystals that align well with it are carnelian, amber, and calcite.

- **Solar Plexus Chakra (Manipura).** The solar plexus chakra is located between the navel and the ribs, and governs the intestines. Manipura is associated with self-esteem, will, and manifestation. Its color is yellow, and it aligns best with citrine, topaz, and tiger's eye.

- **Heart Chakra (Anahata).** The heart chakra is located in the center of the chest, governing the heart and lungs. It's associated with universal love, openness, and compassion. Its color is green, and crystals that align best with it are malachite, rose quartz, and green or pink tourmaline.

- **Throat Chakra (Vishuddha).** The throat chakra is located on the throat, and governs both the voice and the ears. It's associated with communication, self-expression, and truth. Its color is blue, and it works well with lapis lazuli, sodalite, and aquamarine.

- **Third Eye Chakra (Ajna).** The third eye chakra is located in the center of the forehead, and governs the brain, head, and eyes. It's associated with vision, intuition, and knowledge. Its color is purple, and crystals that align best with it are amethyst, azurite, and alexandrite.

- **The Crown Chakra (Sahasrara).** The crown chakra is located at the top of the head, and governs the connection to divinity. It's associated with enlightenment, fulfillment, and completion. Its color is white or indigo, and the crystals that align with it are clear quartz, selenite, and celestite.

The chakra system is ancient and requires deep study to fully understand all that is involved. A skilled crystal healer will have extensive knowledge of the chakras. Through techniques like laying of the hands, sound therapy, and more, they're able to detect which chakras are overactive and which are underactive. In most people, some chakras become blocked or have a leakage. For example, signs of a dim or underactive throat chakra can manifest as throat and ear problems, extreme shyness, or avoiding social contact. An overactive throat chakra could result in saying inappropriate things, or an inability to control the impulse to rant, interrupt, or speak without thought.

Crystals can be placed on chakras to treat over or under activation, remove blockages, or clear out impurities. The energetic field of each crystal is different and aligns with the chakra in various ways, including through color. In a crystal healing session, a crystal is typically placed on each of the chakras to stabilize and balance them. The crystal vibrates with life energy, or prana, and acts as medicine to the chakra.

In addition to the physical placement of crystals on the body, sometimes a crystal grid will be placed around the person being treated to direct energy, bring protection, or sanctify the space so healing can take place.

Reiki

Reiki is a Japanese healing practice developed in the 1800s. It's commonly referred to as "energy healing," and is practiced by a trained professional, who transfers the energy of the life force through their hands into the patient.

The word Reiki comes from the Japanese word 'Rei,' which means universal, and 'ki,' which means life energy. When energy stagnates in the body from physical or emotional pain it can result in illness. A Reiki practitioner will channel life energy into the affected areas to clear them and resume a balanced flow of energy in the physical, mental, and spiritual spheres. They direct this energy through their own bodies into the patient, acting as a conduit. Many people report feeling intense heat or pulses of energy coming from the hands of a Reiki master when receiving treatment.

Traditional Reiki requires a practitioner to complete several levels of study and practice to become a Reiki master. In recent years, other forms of Reiki have developed that don't have this prerequisite.

Not all Reiki practitioners make use of crystals, but in recent years an overlap has developed between Reiki, chakra therapy, and crystal healing. Some practitioners combine all three, while others use crystals only in long-distance Reiki sessions to direct and send healing energy.

Reiki is performed for many reasons. It's been used to treat stress and anxiety, migraines, and even cancer.

For those who do choose to include crystals in their Reiki practice, the reasons are similar to that of chakra healers: they direct life energy into affected areas. Crystals are sometimes placed on the body during a Reiki session, held in the patient's hand, or placed in a grid around them. If you'd like to learn more about the history and practice of Reiki, I have a book dedicated solely to that topic, entitled "Reiki: A Beginner's Guide to Energy Healing." You can find the book simply by entering the title on Amazon.

Crystal Elixirs

An elixir is a liquid medicinal solution. You may have recently seen water bottles for sale that have a crystal embedded in them; these are meant to create crystal elixirs.

Crystals can be placed in water to imbue it with the traits specific to the crystal, either for healing or for manifesting. As a crystal sits in the water, it transfers its energy into the liquid. When the liquid is consumed, the vibrations of the crystal are absorbed by the body. You can create crystal elixirs for almost any purpose, such as stress reduction, to treat headaches or insomnia, or to manifest love or prosperity.

How to make a crystal elixir

Make absolutely certain not to include toxic crystals in an elixir, and be aware that some crystals will be damaged by water. There are lists of these in chapter six.

1. Select a crystal based on its healing and manifesting properties.
2. Cleanse and charge the crystal.
3. Place the crystal in a glass jar and pour drinkable water over it.
4. Leave the mixture in the sunlight for one day.
5. Drink the water.

If you want to create an elixir with a crystal that can't be put in water, you can seal the crystal in an airtight jar, place the jar in a bowl, and then pour the water over the jar, following the above directions. The vibrations of the crystal will still enter the water, without ruining your crystal.

Some elixirs include alcohol and natural preservatives, so they can be stored and used for longer periods of time. These are usually added to water a couple of drops at a time and then consumed.

An alternative way to use a crystal elixir is to put it in a spray bottle and mist yourself or the space around you with crystal essence.

Crystals and Manifestation

We've discussed the healing power of crystals, but only touched on the concept of manifestation.

Crystals attract or repel various energy, beyond just healing the body or mind. Some are believed to bring loving energy into a space, some promote peace, and some can create a shield of energetic protection. As you read through the crystal descriptions in chapter three, you'll discover just how many uses crystals have.

A basic way to use a crystal in manifesting is to cleanse and program it, and then simply carry it with you. It will attract more of its existing energy to you. This is why some people are very intentional about which gemstone jewelry they wear. If they're wearing sodalite, it could be because they want to manifest good communication skills. If they have a citrine bracelet, they might be manifesting joy.

Crystal grids use a combination of multiple crystals and sacred geometry to attract or manifest desires. Some people create grids in the home for protection, to induce peace, or to attract love or wealth.

Chapter 2: Working with Crystals

When you begin your study of crystals, it can be overwhelming. There's a lot to learn, such as how to cleanse and charge them, what all the different shapes mean, and what each different crystal accomplishes. This chapter will teach you all about choosing the right crystals for your purpose and how to care for them.

Cleansing and Charging

You've probably come across references to cleansing and charging crystals, and perhaps noticed that people put them under the moon at certain times.

Cleansing and charging a crystal means to clear its energetic field of all unwanted debris, and then charge it with power. This is necessary to access the strongest, purest form of a crystal's energy.

Cleansing

Crystals are sensitive to all the vibrations they come in contact with. A crystal that has been used for healing can absorb negativity or illness. A gem that has been sitting in a shop for months, handled by many people, will take on energy from each individual. A crystal that's been forgotten in a drawer for a long time will become stagnant and need a bit of refreshing. Cleansing crystals clears away all of this extra energy so that the stone's energy will vibrate strong and clear. There are various methods for doing this, as detailed below.

- **Water.** This might seem obvious since most things are cleaned with water, but when it comes to crystals, there's more to it than just rinsing them under the tap. You can cleanse your crystals with water by placing them in a bowl, covering them with water, and letting them sit for a few hours. This allows the water to gently draw the accumulated energy from the crystal. The second way to use water is through natural sources. You can carefully place your crystals in a pond or stream (only if you know they won't be swept away!), gather rainwater to put them in, or place them outside while it's raining. Crystals react well to untreated water sources because they share the same natural life energy.

- **Salt.** Sea salt is known for its antibacterial properties. It plays a similar role when it comes to crystal cleansing. Put your crystals in a bowl and cover them with sea salt. Allow them to sit for a few hours. The salt will draw off unwanted energy and ground it. Remember, some crystals can be damaged by salt, which are listed in chapter six.

- **Earth.** The earth is where all life begins and ends. It's a very powerful thing! Placing crystals in the ground realigns them with the earth's energy, which is almost like tucking them in for a rejuvenating nap. Place your crystals in a shallow hole in the ground, and cover them with dirt. Be sure to mark the spot. After a few hours, dig them up. If you can't do this, you can simply fill a container with dirt, and put the crystal in it.

- **Selenite.** Selenite is a mineral, often referred to as a crystal, that is known to both cleanse and charge other crystals simultaneously. Place it on top of your crystal and in a few hours your crystal will be cleansed and charged. You can purchase disks made of selenite for placing multiple crystals on for cleansing.

- **Smoke.** Burning herbs or incense is a well-known way to clear a crystal's energy field. Pass the stone through the smoke to purify it.

Charging

Once your crystal has been purified, it needs to be charged, kind of like a battery. A crystal has its own power and vibration at all times, but charging it will strengthen those inherent properties. Like cleansing, there are many ways to do this, most of them involving nature.

- **Moonlight.** Moonlight is by far the most popular way to charge crystals. The full moon is when lunar energies are at their brightest and most powerful. Placing crystals outdoors in the light of the full moon will empower them and enhance their properties.

- **Sunlight.** Just as the sun empowers all of life to grow and thrive, the same can be said for crystals. Place your crystals in direct sunlight for a few hours to amp up their energy. Remember that some crystals fade in direct sun, so be sure to keep an eye on them.

- **Quartz Points.** Clear quartz crystal conducts and directs energy. Place several quartz points around your crystal, with their points turned toward it. The quartz will draw power and direct it into the crystal, filling it with energy.

Programming

Programming a crystal, sometimes called empowering, is taking all of that amazing power in your cleansed, charged crystal and giving it a destination—kind of like giving it a job.

Programming is simple. Hold your cleansed, charged crystal in your hand. Visualize the thing you want it to do. If you are seeking healing, visualize yourself fully healed. If it's peace you're seeking, see yourself in your most tranquil state. As you imagine the situation exactly how you wish it to be, you're sending emotions and vibrations into the crystal that align with your intention. The crystal will then attract more of the same. You can do this several times if you like. Every time you look at the crystal, you'll think of your goal, further aligning it, and yourself, with a successful outcome.

Once a crystal has been cleansed, charged, and programmed, it can be carried in your pocket, worn as jewelry, placed in the home, or included in a grid.

Any time you feel the crystal's vibration becoming weak, you can repeat the empowerment process.

Choosing Your Crystals

When there's so much to choose from, it's difficult to know where to begin your crystal collection. There's no need to purchase huge amounts of expensive, rare stones, or feel like you need to buy every different shape available (although both of those things are tempting). You can start simple, with just a few common gems like quartz, agates, or jaspers. You can purchase these online or at a metaphysical shop, usually for a reasonable price. Even common, inexpensive crystals are powerful things! So just pick one and see what happens.

When you receive your crystals, first cleanse and empower them, and then take some time getting to know each one. Carry it with you for the day and take note of how you feel. Was your mood different? Did it seem like certain situations were attracted to you? Was your environment more peaceful than usual? It can be helpful to keep a journal of each stone you work with, taking notes about how they make you feel or the experiences you have.

Over time you'll discover that just like everything, you have a preference for certain crystals. You might even discover there are a couple you just don't vibe with, and that's okay too.

Crystal Shapes

As you shop around, you'll notice that crystals are cut into tons of different shapes. There's everything from hearts, to wands, to animals. Some crystals are cut just for decoration, but others have a meaningful purpose.

- **Wands.** Wands are long and smooth, usually with a point at one end. These are used in healing to direct energy to a specific spot on the body. The energy of the crystal is condensed in the point and directed into the area where it is needed.

- **Spheres**. Spheres are best known for telling the future. They're used in a practice called 'scrying', which is a form of divination. A ball-shaped crystal emits energy equally in all directions. This creates a generous, consistent flow of energy, making it good for impacting a large space.

- **Cube.** A cube-shaped crystal promotes stability and grounding.

- **Pyramid.** Pyramid-shaped crystals work two ways. They can attract universal life energy to their point and then draw down to their base, thus bringing the energy to earthly life. They can also send energy, by gathering it at the base and then transmitting it out through the tip. Pyramids are excellent for placing in the center of crystal grids.

- **Tower.** Crystal towers are also favored for grids. They are a tall structure that comes to a point at the top. These work in a similar fashion as a pyramid.

- **Single point.** A crystal with a point on one end can occur naturally or be hand cut. When pointed away from the body, it pulls energy out. When pointed towards the body, it brings energy in. For example, in the case of a headache, it would be pointed outward, away from the body to remove the pain. In the case of a broken heart, it would be pointed towards the body to direct energy to the problem for healing.

- **Double point.** A crystal with points at both ends radiates energy in two directions at once and can help create balance.

- **Oval.** A crystal shaped like a flattened oval is sometimes known as a worry stone. These oval stones fit neatly in the palm of your hand and are used to induce tranquility, reduce stress, or can be held during meditation.

- **Animals and other carved shapes.** You can find crystals cut into almost any shape. There are cats, owls, skulls, hearts, and more. These shapes don't necessarily have a function and are mainly decorative.

Crystal Colors

One of the reasons that specific crystals align with each chakra is because of the power of color. Just like sound, each color has a unique vibration. These vibrations attract or repel certain energies. Crystal colors are useful not only in chakra healing but in manifesting as well. This is partially due to the personal associations that you make with each color; if you find light blue peaceful, a crystal in that hue will be all the more effective for your peace-inducing crystal grid. Your personal preference, combined with its inherent qualities, will strengthen a crystal's manifesting power.

- **Red.** Passion, sexuality, carnality

- **Orange.** Success, joy, creativity

- **Yellow.** Inspiration, manifestation, personal power

- **Green.** Growth, abundance, wealth

- **Blue.** Empathy, nurturance, healing

- **Purple.** Intuition, psychic ability, wisdom

- **Black.** Protection, stability, shielding

- **White.** Spirituality, purification, cleansing

- **Clear.** Universal power, life force, vision

- **Brown.** Grounding, balance, practicality

- **Pink.** Love, friendship, gentleness

Other Variables

Size. Many people equate size with power, leading them to believe they need to obtain monstrous chunks of crystal to keep in their homes to influence the atmosphere. While large crystals are certainly beautiful, don't worry if you don't have access to them; few people do. A crystal the size of your pinky contains the same power as a large specimen. The energy of a large stone might feel slightly more overpowering in a physical sense, but when it comes to manifestation, size doesn't matter.

Raw or polished. Crystals are available in both rough chunks and polished specimens. The polished version is often brighter in color, and visually impactful, while some people feel the rough form is more natural and therefore powerful. Some people feel that a stone that's been cut and changed from its natural state is somehow tainted. Some people will only work with natural crystal points, rather than points created by cutting. This is truly a matter of preference and something to decide on your own as you progress through your learning.

Dyed stones. Another thing that brings about differences in opinion is dyed stones. Some crystals, like turquoise, are sometimes dyed to brighten their color. The crystal is still real turquoise, but it's been subjected to human intervention. Some crystal enthusiasts feel this interferes with its healing and manifestation power. Again, this is open to opinion and preference.

Storing crystals. When you're not using your crystals, wrap them in soft cloth to protect them from dust and damage. Keep them in a safe place. If you're displaying them, be sure to cleanse and charge them every so often so they don't become dormant.

Chapter 3: Crystal Properties

Here you'll find an alphabetical list of various crystals and minerals, along with a description of their healing components and metaphysical properties. This list will help you understand the crystal grids described in chapter five, and give you guidance in creating your own crystal healing remedies down the road.

Agate

Agate comes in many colors and patterns, including bands, mottling, and veining. While the different colors bring varying attributes, they all share some commonalities.

Healing: Agate is a balancing stone that stabilizes the aura. It can be placed over the heart to remove blockages or emotional pain. Agate is good for digestion, and can be included in an elixir to help with gastrointestinal issues. Agate can be worn or carried to help with concentration, emotional stability, and bring a general sense of grounding.

Manifesting: Agates are associated with the protection of the self and can be worn or carried in situations where you feel vulnerable. The different colors correlate with various goals.

- **Black**. Protects the self and property
- **Blue lace**. Heals shame, inducing gentleness and self-love
- **Fire agate**. Ignites the potential to achieve goals and dreams

- **Moss agate**. Attracts prosperity and financial stability
- **Tree agate**. Stimulates personal and spiritual growth

Amazonite

Amazonite is a soft bluish-green color, and acts as a filter in many ways. It is believed to absorb cell phone emanations and other forms of electromagnetic pollution. Mentally, it filters incoming information to help organize one's thoughts.

Healing: Amazonite soothes the nervous system and helps bring calmness. It helps with deficiencies that cause tooth decay and osteoporosis. It is used to gently deal with trauma and to alleviate fear.

Manifesting: Amazonite is a stone of creativity that opens the doors to inspiration and opportunity. It inspires creative people with fresh ideas and manifests universal love.

Amber

While amber is often called a crystal, it's actually fossilized tree resin that can take millennia to form. This gives it powerful earthing energy.

Healing: Amber has been used to alleviate depression and help bring about positivity in its place. It absorbs pain and negativity, allowing healing to flourish. It can treat some throat problems, joint issues, and is sometimes considered an antibiotic.

Manifesting: Due to its old age, amber can help people connect to their ancestral past and help heal generational trauma. It promotes a sunny, positive outlook, encourages creative thinking, and promotes wisdom.

Amethyst

Healing: Amethyst aids digestion and elimination, and boosts the immune system. It releases tension and can ease headaches. It also reduces swelling, bruising, and skin conditions. Amethyst can balance unstable mood swings, aid insomnia, and is often used to treat addiction in conjunction with professional guidance. It repels anger, fear, and insecurity.

Manifesting: Amethyst is associated with psychic ability, and can be placed on the third eye chakra to increase one's psychic vision. It can also be kept in the bedroom to protect against nightmares.

Angelite

Angelite gets its name from its connection to the angelic realm.

Healing: Angelite opens the mind and heightens one's perceptivity to energetic healing. It can help a person learn to communicate effectively by increasing empathy. Angelite is often used to initiate the process of spiritual rebirth.

Manifesting: Angelite enhances telepathy and spiritual communication. It can also help a person connect with their astrological sign and planetary influences.

Aquamarine

Aquamarine is associated with water because of its pale blue color. It was once carried by sailors to protect them against drowning.

Healing: Aquamarine is cleansing, like the water it's named after. It can regulate hormones, help with sore throats, and act as a tonic for cleansing the body's organs. It can be used to soothe fear, clarify the mind, and help bring closure to unresolved issues. It banishes patterns of self-destruction. Aquamarine is a good meditation crystal because it induces higher states of consciousness and can be placed on the body to cleanse the aura.

Manifesting: Aquamarine can help manifest emotional understanding and balance. It can be used to protect against negative energies.

Calcite

A piece of calcite placed in a room can cleanse negative energy from the environment.

Healing: Calcite accelerates the healing process and encourages quick growth. It aids with spiritual development. It creates a bridge between feelings and intellect, resulting in emotional intelligence. It's also said to increase memory. Calcite strengthens the skeleton by promoting calcium uptake. As an elixir, calcite can help with skin conditions and minor wounds.

Manifesting: There are many colors of calcite that can help manifest various things. Pink promotes love, blue embraces healing energy, and green attracts wealth and abundance.

Carnelian

Carnelian is a fiery stone that contains the power of the sun. Its bright orange color encompasses passion, joy, and inspiration.

Healing: Carnelian boosts vitality and increases motivation. It treats lethargy and hopelessness and promotes courage. Carnelian boosts the metabolism and is believed to increase fertility. It helps the body absorb nutrients and induces healthy blood flow. Carnelian can assist with banishing resentment and envy, making room for joy.

Manifesting: Carnelian manifests joy, love of life, positivity, and success. Its fiery energy stokes one's passion to reach their goals, accelerating the journey to victory.

Chalcedony

Some ancient civilizations drank from chalices made of chalcedony and silver to protect against poisoning. It is also said to improve the bond between mother and child.

Healing: Chalcedony increases lactation in nursing mothers. It also encourages self-reflection, which brings inner healing. It harmonizes the body, mind, and soul, leading to self-actualization. It's also said to transform sadness into joy through its cleansing capabilities.

Manifesting: Chalcedony increases benevolence and generosity. It also creates harmony within groups of people, making it excellent to keep in the workplace or other community spaces where many different personalities come together.

Chrysocolla

Chrysocolla is said to represent discretion and diplomacy. It's a stone of tranquility, and removes negative energy from people and places.

Healing: Chrysocolla can heal relationship problems, both within an individual and as a couple. It helps boost inner fortitude and the ability to accept change. It can be used to deconstruct and eliminate harmful emotional patterns. It also treats muscle spasms, detoxes the liver and kidneys, and lowers blood pressure.

Manifesting: Chrysocolla promotes wisdom and discernment. It promotes seeing and telling the truth, and banishing lies and dishonesty. It can be used to manifest honest, open communication in all areas of life.

Citrine

Citrine is a solid golden color. Often, amethyst is heat-treated and sold as citrine. You can recognize false citrine because it's usually white or clear on the bottom and dark yellow on top.

Healing: Citrine encourages warmth, cheer, and energy. It can help unblock communication issues in an individual and increase self-confidence. It can release the past, helping someone see the brightness of the future. It brings inner calm and wisdom, which helps with decision making.

Manifesting: Citrine encourages abundance in all areas of life: love, wealth, and peace. It strengthens one's ability to reach their goals. As a stone of success and positivity, its energy is useful in almost any crystal grid.

Emerald

While cut emerald makes for expensive jewelry, rough emerald is far more accessible, reasonably priced, and readily available.

Healing: Emerald aids in recovery from illness or emotional trauma. It helps address negative behaviors and replace them with positive action. Emerald can help someone maintain strength to overcome hardship. It alleviates rheumatism and detoxes the liver. It's also associated with eye health.

Manifesting: Emerald is said to encourage a loving, happy home life. It manifests unconditional love in all its forms and encourages loyalty. It brings balance to relationships.

Fluorite

Fluorite comes in a range of colors including purple, turquoise, green, and clear, but it may fade if left in the sunlight.

Healing: Fluorite protects against the electromagnetic fields emitted by various technologies, so keep some with your device. When used in healing, fluorite draws stress out of the body and aura, while simultaneously cleansing and purifying. Fluorite then organizes and aligns unbalanced or scattered energy. Fluorite creates an organized, logical mind, helping separate emotions from intellect.

Manifesting: Fluorite can manifest increased learning capacity. It brings structure to chaotic situations and dispels misplaced emotions. It also supports creativity and productivity.

Garnet

Garnet, like emerald, can be expensive as jewelry but is more affordable in its rough state. This blood-red gem is among the oldest in the world, and has been unearthed in Egyptian tombs.

Healing: Garnet is helpful for problems of the blood, heart, and lungs. It strengthens the physical body and stamina, and increases the libido. Garnet helps let go of limiting beliefs and unwanted patterns of behavior. It can heal anger directed at the self, and fortify survival instincts.

Manifesting: Garnet is a stone of loyalty and devotion in love, and can help you find long-term relationships. It attracts vitality to any situation, and can strengthen your resolve during challenging situations.

Hematite

A manufactured material called "hemalyke" is often sold as jewelry to replace real hematite. It looks the same but isn't natural. Hematite does have magnetic properties, but rarely as strong as the hemalyke magnets that are sold.

Healing: Hematite is a strongly grounding stone. It aligns body, mind, and spirit, and keeps a person anchored in reality. It can help treat anemia, and stimulates the formation of red blood cells. Hematite can increase focus and concentration, keeping thoughts in the here and now instead of worrying about the unknown.

Manifesting: Hematite is said to be helpful in legal issues. Being magnetic, it can be used to attract specific energy. On its own, it attracts will-power and confidence.

Iron Pyrite

Iron Pyrite is a shimmering mineral known as "fool's gold." It looks so similar to actual gold that throughout history many miners were tricked into thinking they'd struck it rich upon finding it.

Healing: Iron pyrite creates a strong energetic field around a person. It prevents energy from being siphoned away. It can treat fatigue and boost oxygen in the blood. It is known for helping get to the root of a problem and drawing it to the surface to be healed.

Manifesting: Iron pyrite is said to attract money and gambler's luck. It's also carried to give the impression of confidence and competence.

Jasper

Jasper is associated with nurturance. It comes in many colors and patterns, all of them reducing stress and promoting stability.

Healing: Jasper supports sexual organ function and increases sexual pleasure. It helps keep minerals balanced in the body. It protects the physical and energetic bodies from environmental stress and helps bring level-headedness in times of conflict. It can bring a sense of safety to those who feel vulnerable.

Manifesting: Jasper helps turn dreams and ideas into action. Strongly connected to earth energy, it is a practical, stable stone. It can aid in bringing practicality and reason to one's life, helping fulfill one's basic needs.

Kyanite

Kyanite can be blue, white, pink, green, or black. Sometimes it has pearlized areas, giving it a unique sheen. Kyanite can't hold onto negative energy, and therefore never needs to be cleansed.

Healing: Kyanite is a natural pain reliever that helps heal infections and lower fevers. It enhances meditation experiences and increases intuition. Kyanite can help guide a person through the grieving process. Kyanite destroys blockages, releasing self-expression and the ability to speak the truth.

Manifesting: Kyanite can help stimulate meaningful dreams and increase psychic ability. It connects the mind to the higher levels of spirituality or divinity.

Labradorite

Labradorite is named for its origins in Labrador, Newfoundland, in Northeast Canada. Labradorite is a dark tone with rainbows shimmering within it, reminiscent of the northern lights.

Healing: Labradorite can calm an overactive imagination. It can help understand one's spiritual purpose and can stimulate psychic ability. It protects the aura from the thoughts and projections of others. It can bring up repressed memories that need to be released.

Manifesting: Labradorite can be included in the quest for esoteric knowledge. It opens the door to life's mysteries and reveals the great secrets of the cosmos.

Lapis Lazuli

Lapis lazuli is a blue crystal that contains flecks of iron pyrite.

Healing: Lapis lazuli helps fight migraines and alleviates depression. It boosts the immune system, and can help treat vertigo and insomnia. It can be placed on the body to release stress. Lapis lazuli reveals one's inner truth, which will guide them to spiritual enlightenment.

Manifesting: Lapis lazuli will reveal the truth during times of confusion and help the mind accept it with objectivity. It promotes compassion and nobility in action. It manifests wisdom and maturity.

Malachite

Malachite is toxic and should never be ingested in any form, including elixirs. In polished form or set in jewelry, it is harmless. However, in raw form, or while being processed and producing dust, it is dangerous to inhale or get on the skin.

Healing: Malachite absorbs pollutants from the body and the environment. It should be cleansed after every use. Malachite clears and activates the energy centers of the body. It helps ease menstrual cramps and facilitates childbirth. Because it amplifies both positive and negative energy, it should be handled with caution.

Manifesting: Malachite brings on big changes and is useful while going through major transitions in life. It can destroy the old to bring in the new.

Moldavite

Moldavite was formed when a meteorite struck the earth in what we now know as Germany, millions of years ago. A crater still exists there. There is only so much moldavite in the world, which makes it a little more expensive than other crystals.

Healing: Moldavite helps highly sensitive people function with the difficulties of earthly life. It helps the spirit connect to the body, and can reveal the best path for the future during times of confusion. It can reveal one's life's purpose and the reason they're incarnated at this time.

Manifesting: Because of how it was formed, moldavite unites the celestial with the earthly. It connects a person to their highest self and initiates deep spiritual experiences. It can help you see symbols and synchronicities that are meaningful to your life's path.

Moonstone

Moonstone gets its name from its luminous, mystical sheen. It's closely connected to emotions, which wax and wane like the moon.

Healing: Moonstone aids digestion and eliminates fluid retention. It's used to treat PMS, and aids in pregnancy, childbirth, and breastfeeding. It's also sometimes used to treat insomnia. It can soothe overly emotional reactiveness and reduce feelings of aggression.

Manifesting: Moonstone can help induce prophetic dreams and increase psychic abilities. It helps people get in touch with their vulnerability, and promotes emotional expression.

Obsidian

Obsidian is volcanic glass formed when molten lava meets cold air or water. In ancient times it was often made into knives and arrows.

Healing: Obsidian can help with acceptance of difficult issues which is a step towards healing from the past. It dissolves tension and cramps. Obsidian exposes underlying or suppressed trauma so it can be faced and resolved. It can help access past lives to find insight into current issues. It detects weaknesses and blockages in the aura.

Manifesting: Black obsidian is associated with psychic ability, and is often used for divination. It can bring about abrupt change, which is useful for those who are seeking big life transformations of any kind. It is carried as a protection charm.

Onyx

The most common type of onyx is black, but it is available in other colors like gray, blue, brown, and yellow. It is believed to absorb the memories and experiences of those who carry it.

Healing: Onyx can benefit teeth and bones as well as those with blood disorders. It provides a stabilizing effect during times of stress. It promotes personal confidence and strength, as well as general stamina. Onyx can be used to detect past injuries that are currently impacting the body and spirit. It is also used to heal grief.

Manifesting: Onyx brings strength and offers protection. It can help create a connection to a higher power and understand one's destiny. It is an excellent stone to protect yourself from the thoughts and feelings of others.

Opal

Opals are easily obtained, but in gem form can be expensive. Try to seek out rough or lower grade opal. The monetary value of opal doesn't impact its healing or manifestation qualities.

Healing: Opal helps release inhibitions surrounding emotions, opening the way to honest communication. It helps those who struggle to face their own feelings. Dark-colored opal can help with childbirth and alleviate menstrual issues.

Manifesting: Opal induces mystical visions, and can be worn or carried when seeking answers to life's bigger questions. It attracts love, desire, and sensuality. It encourages feelings of lightheartedness and a spontaneous spirit. It helps bring inner beauty to the surface and encourages self-love.

Peridot

Peridot is usually a translucent olive-green color, but sometimes has a brown or red tinge. Stones are usually quite small.

Healing: Peridot cleanses toxins in the body and clears the mind of negativity. Peridot can be used to help break obsessions or free a person of guilt they are hanging on to. It can also help alleviate jealousy, envy, and resentment to create room for feelings of confidence and forgiveness.

Manifesting: Peridot's green color connects it to growth, prosperity, and abundance. It can attract wealth and material success. It has also been used for protection against evil spirits.

Prehnite

Yellowish-green prehnite sometimes has an interesting surface that looks like bubbles. It's formed in South Africa, and is easily obtained world-wide.

Healing: Prehnite helps repair connective tissue in the body and can treat blood disorders. Prehnite encourages spiritual growth for seekers, opening them to higher states of consciousness. It helps alleviate nightmares and deep-seated fears, and can release someone from a "lack mentality."

Manifesting: Prehnite helps connect to divine energies, drawing their influence to wherever it is placed. It calms any environment it's in, which makes it excellent for including in crystal grids in the home or workspace. It promotes abundance in all areas of life, so it can be paired with other crystals to increase their power.

Quartz

Quartz crystal is the most useful crystal in your arsenal. It amplifies and directs energy, and increases the power of all other crystals. It is often used in crystal grids for all kinds of purposes because of its unique power. It comes in many colors which are used for various applications.

Healing: Quartz can be used to treat any condition of mind, body, or spirit. It promotes balance and boosts the immune system. Quartz points are used in healing the body by guiding energy directly to the afflicted area.

Manifesting: Quartz crystal raises energy to its highest potential, making it a must-have in all applications. Quartz aids meditation, enhances spiritual awareness, and is useful for manifestation due to its amplification abilities. The different colors of quartz have varying associations:

- **Pink (known as rose quartz)**. Attracts all forms of love, including romantic, self-love, family love, and friendship
- **Blue**. Inspires hope and serenity
- **Orange (tangerine quartz)**. Heals past life trauma
- **Rutilated**. Facilitates mediumship and divination
- **Smoky**. Promotes positive thinking and stress reduction

Rhodochrosite

Rhodochrosite is a pink stone with lacy designs and bands. It's associated with all forms of attraction and love.

Healing: Rhodochrosite normalizes blood pressure and stimulates the sex organs. It can enhance feelings of self-worth, aid those struggling with denial, and eases a broken heart.

Manifesting: Rhodochrosite attracts all kinds of sexual and intimate relations. Use it in grids or wear it as jewelry when hoping to find a partner.

Selenite

Selenite is another must-have gem, and is easily obtained. It's best known for cleansing and charging any crystal it touches, and therefore never has to be cleansed or charged itself. It's readily available in raw form, cut shapes, tumbled stones, and is even made into lamps.

Healing: Selenite promotes clarity of mind. It cleanses the aura and removes unwanted negative energy that may have attached itself to a person. It reverses the effects of free radicals and encourages a nurturing attitude.

Manifesting: Selenite is believed to connect to divine beings, particularly angels. It creates a bridge between the physical and ethereal realms. It can be placed in the home to prevent unwanted energies from entering, and to create a peaceful vibration throughout.

Sodalite

Sodalite is deep blue with white veining. It's found in igneous rock in volcanic debris. It's often confused with lapis lazuli because they appear so similar.

Healing: Sodalite unites logic and intuition, which helps a person understand their circumstances and allows them to be true to themselves. It eliminates confusion, encouraging rationality and clear perception. It stimulates fluid absorption in the body and can help with insomnia. It comforts those with trust issues, allowing them to become open to friendship and community.

Manifesting: Sodalite encourages communication and resolution of conflict. It strengthens feelings of trust and camaraderie among a group, making it perfect for any situation that requires teamwork.

Sunstone

Sunstone contains the qualities of the sun, inspiring warmth, joy, and growth. Some sunstone contains flecks of hematite, making it especially good for attracting energy.

Healing: Sunstone can help lift depression and encourage a love of life. It can cleanse the aura of the influence of other people's thoughts and actions. It helps reduce codependency and increases independence. Sunstone can help someone believe in their own strengths.

Manifesting: Sunstone is associated with good fortune. It can be carried to stoke the inner fire, destroying darkness inside. It attracts self-love and personal empowerment. It also attracts positive attention, making it useful in seeking employment or getting your work noticed.

Tiger's Eye

Tiger's eye has shiny golden stripes with bands of dark brown. Due to its coloring, it is said to contain both the power of the sun and the earth.

Healing: Tiger's eye treats eye ailments and increases night vision. It can ground someone who lives in a fantasy land, helping them get in touch with real life. It helps people understand their own true wants, needs, and intentions.

Manifesting: Tiger's eye can reveal the truth and inspire honesty. It attracts integrity and helps achieve goals. It is a stone of success and determination.

Tourmaline

Tourmaline is available in a wide range of colors, which all share some basic properties. Tourmaline wands are often used by healers to balance the chakras and clear the aura.

Healing: Tourmaline increases energy flow and removes blockages. It protects against electromagnetic smog and radiation. It grounds and stabilizes, helps develop a positive attitude, and removes negative energy from the body. It can guard sensitive people against being overwhelmed by the thoughts and actions of others.

Manifesting: Tourmaline protects against being victimized by others with bad intentions. It forms an energetic shield around a person. It also encourages fidelity and honesty in relationships.

Turquoise

Turquoise is said to become drained of color when it has absorbed the negativity of a person, or to change color when danger is near. Sometimes a stone called howlite is dyed to imitate turquoise.

Healing: Turquoise is said to heal the whole body from head to toe, enhancing the immune system. It is anti-inflammatory and detoxifying. It releases inhibitions that are holding someone back, combats self-sabotage, and stabilizes mood.

Manifesting: Turquoise is believed to be a truly masterful stone. It attracts luck, wealth, love, and joy. It can also strengthen one's tie to the earth and the environment.

Unakite

Unakite is a green and pink stone that resonates with animal lovers.

Healing: Unakite promotes a healthy pregnancy and regulates the reproductive system. It encourages a sense of calm. Unakite helps people to address the past and integrate it into meaningful lessons, encouraging psychological growth.

Manifesting: Unakite can increase a person's connection to animals and nature. It is said to increase awareness of the spirit within all living things, especially trees and plants.

Chapter 4: Crystal Grids

A crystal grid is a collection of gems arranged in a specific pattern to attract and focus the universal life energy towards a specified end. Creating a crystal grid involves several factors for success: choosing crystals that work together harmoniously, understanding their placement on the grid, and choosing which grid works best for your goal.

Sacred Geometry

Since the dawn of the universe, all things in existence have been created from the same basic shapes and mathematical patterns. The universe and all of creation continuously expand, following natural laws of replication. This ongoing expansion is what fuels existence.

If you look at the bottom of a pine cone or the center of a sunflower, you can see this phenomenon at work in the form of an ever-expanding, self-replicating spiral shape. This mathematical sequence, known as the golden ratio, is exactly the same in some houseplants as it is in galaxies in outer space. This demonstrates that all of creation is based on a few mathematical sequences, creating all matter. It's amazing! The same energies and structures exist in all things from the stars to the dirt beneath our feet, composed of repeating shapes and patterns. This is called sacred geometry.

Everything in the universe can be reduced to five geometric shapes, known as the five platonic solids. These are the pyramid, cube, octahedron, icosahedron, and tetrahedron. All of these shapes have identical facets, equal polygons meeting at each angle, and will fit perfectly within a circle. Even extremely complex organisms like animals and people are built with the same shapes as everything else, and we're sustained by the same life force. These three-dimensional shapes, when drawn flat on a two-dimensional surface, are used to create crystal grids.

Crystal grids based on sacred geometry allow us to tap into the patterns of the universal life force and implement them in our lives. When combined with the power of crystals, we can create a force that expands, attracts, or repels energy based on natural laws and the building blocks of the universe.

Circles

The simple circle is one of the oldest and most powerful symbols. It represents the infinite, never-ending nature of existence. Many crystal grids are made of variations of circle patterns. The circle holds the symbolism of the life cycle, the seasonal cycle, and even the solar and lunar cycles. It signifies perfect completion and wholeness. Circles are inclusive, protective, and unifying.

Vesica Piscis

Vesica piscis refers to two interlocking circles (like a Venn diagram). Many crystal grids include this pattern because it establishes a connection between the divine and the earth. This connection is especially meaningful for manifesting because it creates matter out of thought. Vesica piscis also shows the unity of polar complementary opposites or duality. Duality is fundamental to existence: day and night, light and dark, summer and winter. Both extremes are needed to create balance. Vesica piscis is useful in healing grids and reuniting that which has been separated.

Borromean Rings

Three interlocking circles that evenly overlap one another are known as Borromean rings. They're layered so that if one ring is broken, they will all come apart, signifying strength in unity. The number three is also important as it represents the past, present, and future and is meaningful in many spiritual beliefs (for example, the Holy Trinity).

Tripod of Life

These three interlocking circles are similar to Borromean rings, but the focus is not on the circles themselves. Rather, attention is paid to the interlocking portions of the rings, which form a shape that looks like three flower petals. The tripod of life unites logic, emotion, and spirit, the elements necessary for manifestation. In the very center of the tripod is a triangle with curved sides. Triangles themselves are powerful conduits of energy.

Triangles

Triangles bring together the power of trinity. Mind, body, and spirit, or the past, present and future, and birth, creation, and death. Triangles are included in crystal grids to bring expansion and to enhance energies. They are one of the simplest yet most effective shapes for gridding.

Star of David

The Star of David consists of two perfectly overlapping triangles, one facing up and one facing down, that form a star shape. This symbol is best known as representing the Jewish faith, but it also appears in sacred geometry. In crystal grids, the upward triangle represents the spirit, and the downward triangle represents matter. Unified as a star they become a whole. This illustrates bringing dreams into reality or spirituality into everyday life. It's often used in grids to attract simplicity, love, and peace.

Squares

Squares signify precision, intellect, and knowledge. A square encompasses the many esoteric meanings of the number four: the primal elements of earth, air, fire, and water, the four cardinal directions, and the four seasons. Squares are often included in crystal grids to set boundaries, create realistic thinking, and promote good values. They can build community and restore order to chaotic situations.

Hexagon

The six-sided hexagon is visible within the seed of life and flower of life grids. The hexagon is one of nature's most prevalent building blocks and can be found in beehives, snowflakes, and rock formations. The hexagon is a powerful shape in crystal grids for protection.

Spiral

Spirals appear in nature great and small. Tornadoes and galaxies form spirals, as does our DNA. Spirals form many seashells and are seen in the growth pattern of leaves and flowers. The nature of the spiral is to endlessly expand and grow from one central point. Spirals are used in grids for increasing attraction, or to spread energy far and wide. The Fibonacci spiral, also known as the golden ratio, appears in our bodies, in nature, and the cosmos, building the foundation for much of the universe.

Seed of Life

The seed of life grid is made of seven overlapping circles, encompassed by one large circle. The seed of life grid has a central point of power, surrounded by six identical petals that are perfectly uniform and represent outward expansion. These are unified by a ring. The seed of life contains the power of circles, vesica piscis, and the hexagon.

Flower of Life

The flower of life consists of multiple seeds of life that have expanded and multiplied. Its complicated form includes the Borromean rings, Metatron's cube, hexagons, and the tripod of life. Containing so many forms makes the flower of life a very powerful crystal grid with many uses.

Metatron's Cube

This grid gets its name from the archangel Metatron, who was said to provide a connection to the divine and act as a scribe or recorder of creation. This complex grid contains all five of the platonic solids which means it contains all of the building blocks of the universe. A very powerful pattern, it is also very complicated for those just starting out with crystal gridding as it contains so many lines and patterns.

Creating a Crystal Grid

Crystals aren't just randomly placed on a grid; there is a purpose attached to their placement. Each stone has a different role to play, so to speak. Every grid requires a master stone, way stones, desire stones, and a wand.

The Master Stone

The master stone, sometimes called the focus stone, holds your intention. It is placed in the middle of the grid, and will attract a powerful stream of universal life energy into your grid. Sometimes a crystal tower or pyramid is used because those shapes enhance the focus and intensity of energy. This stone can be aligned with your intention based on its properties. Quartz can take the place of any other crystal and is an excellent master stone. The purpose of the master stone is to absorb life energy and then direct it into the grid, where it will flow through the other stones.

Way Stones

Way stones are placed around the master stone and act as energy conductors. Points are often useful here, as they absorb the powerful energy of the master stone, and then direct and amplify it outwards, however other shapes are fine. You will need a varying number of way stones depending on which grid you're using. The way stones are placed either on the intersecting lines of the grid or in between them. These stones receive the energy from the master stone, further amplifying it and carrying it outwards toward the desire stones.

Desire Stones

Desire stones, which are placed around the perimeter of the grid, should be chosen to represent your goal and align with your intention. These stones will gather the energy streaming from the way stones, giving it a purpose and fine-tuned vibration. These stones take the amplified energy from the way stones and filter it, so to speak, so it vibrates with the frequency of your desire. They send the collective energy of the grid into the world to manifest. Again, the number of these you need depends on which grid you're using.

The Activation Wand

The activation wand can be a quartz point, a hand-cut crystal wand, or a natural selenite wand. Other options are copper wands, a small wooden stick, or even your finger. Once you've arranged your crystals, you will use the wand to trace the lines of the grid from the master stone, outwards. As the wand moves along the pathways of the grid, it connects all the stones and activates the ancient power of sacred geometry.

All of the grid designs are powerful and can be used for almost any goal, but are naturally more aligned with certain energies.

- **Circle.** Belonging, safety, fulfillment, protection
- **Vesica piscis.** Balancing opposites, harmony, compromise, connection
- **Borromean rings.** Family, friends, community, inclusiveness
- **Tripod of life.** New beginnings, birth, fresh starts, initiating projects
- **Triangle.** Serenity, simplicity, peace, spiritual awareness
- **Star of David.** Connecting spirit to matter, balancing the emotions and body
- **Square.** Practicality, vitality, stability, healing, physical health
- **Hexagon.** Protection of self and physical surroundings
- **Spiral.** Increase, gaining momentum, expansion, growth
- **Seed of life.** Success, reaching goals, completion
- **Flower of life.** The inner self, confidence, personal strength, self-love
- **Metatron's cube**. An all-purpose manifesting grid

Making Your Crystal Grid

Before you begin, you must have a clear idea of what you want your crystal grid to accomplish. This can be any goal you currently have, something you'd like to change in your life, or a situation you'd like to occur. This intention will be put into the master stone. There are several ways to imbue the master stone with your objective.

1. **Write an affirmation**. Write your goal down on a piece of paper. Fold it up, and place it underneath the master stone. Your affirmation must be very clear and precise, keeping it to one or two simple sentences. Be sure to avoid negative language, and write your goal as if you already have it. An example of an effective affirmation is "My home is peaceful and secure." An example of an ineffective affirmation would be "Bad energy can't get into my home." The second example focuses on the negative.

2. **Use a photo.** Another way to empower the master stone is to put a picture of your goal beneath it. This can be a printout of a photo you took yourself or something you find online or in a magazine that encompasses your desire. Each time you look at the photo, it reinforces your objective, which pours positive energy into the photo.

3. **Draw a symbol.** Draw a picture of a symbol that aligns with your goal. The symbol might be something very personal that you design yourself, but it can also be generic like a heart for love or a peace sign for tranquility. As you draw the symbol be sure to visualize the desired outcome, imbuing the paper with the power of your thoughts.

Next, choose a grid that appeals to you. There are many free printouts available online, or you can buy one made of wood, stone, or cloth. While each grid is unique, they're all powerful for manifestation in similar ways. The more you work with crystal grids, the more you'll get a feel for which designs you like best.

Once you've decided on a clear intention and chosen your grid, select your crystals. Look at the crystal properties listed in chapter three or use an example from this book.

Select a spot for your crystal grid where it won't be disturbed by pets or children. Choose a quiet time when you won't be interrupted to build your grid.

1. Place the grid on a flat surface. Put your affirmation, symbol, or photo in the center of the grid. Hold your master stone in both hands and press it against your heart. Speak your intention out loud. Visualize your goal as if you already have it. Put your master stone on top of the paper.

2. Place the way stones around it. If they have points, aim them outward. Set them evenly either on the lines of the grid or in the spaces between the lines. As you do this, feel the power of the master stone streaming into each way stone.

3. Place the desire stones around the outside of the grid. Visualize the energy pouring from the sky into the master stone, flowing through the way stones, and filling the desire stones.

4. Hold your wand roughly an inch above the grid. Starting at the center, trace the pattern of the grid. Feel the way the wand creates lines of energy between the stones and along the paths of the ancient symbol. When it's done, spend a moment enjoying the powerful energy you've just created.

After completing your crystal grid, you can continue to empower it every day by using the wand to trace the grid. This further intensifies its energy. You also might enjoy sitting near your crystal grid while visualizing your intention or repeating your affirmation once a day. Every time you do either of these things, you increase its energy as well as your own.

When you've manifested your intention or feel the grid has done its job, gently dismantle it. Cleanse the crystals and put them away until you need them again.

Chapter 5: Sample Crystal Grids

Now it's time to put everything you've learned into practice! Here you'll find some examples of crystal combinations and grids to try yourself. These are just a starting point. After you've experimented with these, you might want to branch out on your own and create personalized grids that are completely unique. You can reference chapter three when deciding on which crystals to include.

Healing Grids

Here is a collection of crystal grids meant to bring healing to various areas of life, on the physical, mental, and spiritual planes.

Simple Balancing Grid

This grid is meant to bring a sense of balance to your inner life. We're all made of both light and dark, positive and negative elements. Rejecting one in favor of the other will create an unhealthy disparity within and result in stress and disharmony. For example, toxic positivity is to completely ignore the shadows, which will cause them to emerge in a disruptive way. Being immersed in a negative mindset, refusing to see any light, is just as damaging. This grid uses the simple vesica piscis grid to integrate your inner light and shadows harmoniously.

Grid: Vesica piscis

Master stone: Quartz

Way stones: Rose quartz

Desire stones: Tree agate

Affirmation: "My light and shadow are balanced and harmonious, bringing me peace and wisdom."

Place the clear quartz in the center of the space where the circles intersect, with the affirmation beneath it. Put rose quartz on the intersecting lines above and below the master stone. Place the remaining two rose quartz in the circles themselves.

Space the agates evenly along the outer circle.

Spend some time with your wand tracing the circles to activate the grid.

Animal Healing Grid

Having an animal friend that is ill or healing from an operation is extremely distressing for them and you. This grid creates healing energy specifically for pets of any kind. You could also put this grid in your backyard to create benevolent energy that attracts birds and other critters.

Grid: Square. A smaller square within a larger one is preferred. You can add an X shape in the middle to connect them.

Master stone: Brown jasper

Way stones: Garnet

Desire stones: Unakite

Affirmation: "My pet (or insert their name) recovers fast and achieves perfect health."

In place of an affirmation, you could use a photo of your pet when they were in premium health. When your animal is healed, cleanse the crystals and store them.

Grid to Heal a Broken Heart

The flower of life grid promotes emotional balance and growth, which are both parts of overcoming heartbreak. This crystal grid will help heal the wounds caused by separation while bolstering personal strength to move on. It also brings the ability to process emotions in a healthy way while keeping grounded.

Grid: Flower of life

Master stone: Fluorite

Way stones: Moonstone

Desire stones: Aquamarine

Affirmation: "My heart is healing in a healthy, balanced way, as I discover my independence."

While dealing with heartbreak, particularly due to a relationship ending, it can be difficult to let go. Often, we're tempted to reach out to the person for the wrong reasons. Any time you feel a desire to engage in this way, go to your grid and use your wand to reactivate it while envisioning your heart filling with healing light.

Grid to Alleviate Grief

Grief following a loss can't be cured overnight, but rather, it is a process that must be worked through over time. During grief, many emotions are drawn to the surface which can be overwhelming. This crystal grid promotes patience during the grieving process while honoring one's feelings, gently leading to acceptance. The grid includes two different desire stones that complement one another. Place them around the grid in an alternating pattern.

Grid: Flower of life

Master stone: Smoky quartz

Way stones: Obsidian

Desire stones: Kyanite and hematite

Affirmation: "I am healthily resolving my grief as I move forward in life."

This grid helps bring healing, but it's also a means of working through your feelings. During grief it's important to acknowledge your emotions, as ignoring or burying them will hinder the process. You can sit in front of this grid while experiencing these feelings, letting yourself cry if needed for release.

Grid to Heal an Illness

While undergoing an illness, a crystal grid can be used in conjunction with the advice and treatment of a medical professional. Place this grid in the space where the person experiencing illness spends most of their time. When crafting the affirmation for this grid, it's important to be very specific.

Grid: Metatron's cube

Master stone: Quartz

Way stones: Garnet

Desire stones: Turquoise

Affirmation: "(Name of person) has healed completely from (name of illness), and is living a healthy, pain-free life."

Every once in a while, visualize the energy from the grid entering into the person you wish to heal, infusing their entire body and mind with bright, nourishing light.

Grid to Alleviate Depression

This grid combines gentle healing energy with a burst of fire and confidence from the carnelian. Create this grid in conjunction with your preferred form of medical attention.

Grid: Star of David

Master stone: Moonstone

Way stones: Carnelian

Desire stones: Lapis lazuli and sunstone

Affirmation: "I am filled with energy, inspiration, and love for life."

In this grid, the Star of David acts as a means to bring the darkness and light into a unified healthy balance. Once united, the polar opposites create healing and invigorating life force.

Chakra Body Grid

A crystal grid doesn't always have to be created on a small flat surface. You can make a grid right on your body to bring healing and balance to your chakra system. This exercise will calm overactive chakras while invigorating sluggish ones. After this healing session, you should feel calm, peaceful, and strong. This process doesn't involve one of the usual grid designs but relies on the actual chakras in your body while implementing the same concepts as gridding. It requires seven stones—one for each chakra—and uses quartz points to direct energy into your body.

For this practice, you will place the appropriate crystal on each chakra, while crystal points direct universal life energy towards them. In your right hand you'll hold black tourmaline for physical grounding, and in your left hand, selenite for aligning with spirit.

This meditation will be done lying down in a peaceful, quiet space where you won't be disturbed.

You will need:

- 1 red jasper placed at the base of the spine
- 1 carnelian placed between the navel and sexual organs
- 1 citrine placed on the solar plexus
- 1 rose quartz placed on the chest
- 1 sodalite placed on the throat
- 1 clear quartz placed near the crown of the head

- 4 or more crystal points. Place these evenly on the floor or bed around your body pointed towards you.
- 1 black tourmaline held in the right hand
- 1 selenite held in the left hand

When you're laying down with the crystals in position, take a few moments to breathe deeply and pay attention to how you feel. You will notice that the energy from the crystals is impacting you in various ways. Usually, there is a light vibration all over the body or a sense of heat. Some crystals might feel heavy, while others seem cool. These sensations are the stones interacting with your chakras.

Visualize the crystal points around you directing streams of universal life energy into the stones on your body.

Now take the following steps to align your chakras:

1. Visualize your root chakra as a spinning red light at the base of your spine. The red jasper is feeding it energy. As you focus on this chakra, say aloud or in your mind, "I am."

2. Next, see your sacral chakra glowing with orange fire. The carnelian upon it invigorates and clears it. State the affirmation, "I feel."

3. Move on to your solar plexus and imagine the citrine crystal fine-tuning its spinning yellow light, making it bright like the sun. State the affirmation, "I manifest."

4. On your heart is the rose quartz, feeding energy into the bright green wheel of your heart chakra. State, "I love."

5. The sodalite crystal placed on your throat opens the blue throat chakra allowing it to expand freely. State the affirmation, "I speak."

6. Bring your attention to your forehead and the third eye chakra. The amethyst pours purple light into this chakra, opening your mind to all that is hidden. State the affirmation, "I know."

7. Last is the crown chakra, which is connected to the quartz crystal. This crown chakra opens like a flower, radiating white light further than you can imagine. State the affirmation, "I am divine."

8. Now all of your chakras are open and vibrating at their peak frequencies. The crystals balance, cleanse, and invigorate them. Visualize the white light of your crown chakra moving down through your body, further brightening the other chakras, strengthening them with universal life energy.

9. Spend as much time here as you like, enjoying the sensation. When you're finished, put these crystals in a special place for next time.

Some people perform this chakra balancing exercise weekly, monthly, or simply any time they aren't feeling their best.

Manifestation Grids

Grid to Manifest Self-Love

Loving the self is the key to a happy life. We're often taught over generations to be very hard on ourselves, whether it's rejecting our own bodies, perceiving our needs as undeserving, or experiencing shame. Once you learn to love yourself and everything about you, the positivity of this radiates outwards and manifests wonderful things.

Grid: Flower of life

Master stone: Rose quartz

Way stones: Blue lace agate

Desire stones: Carnelian and opal

Affirmation: "I am amazing and perfect exactly as I am. I love my body, mind, and spirit."

Everyone struggles with self-love in different ways depending on conditioning, background, and personal experiences. You can tweak the affirmation to specifically address your particular problem.

Prosperity Crystal Grid

This grid is designed to attract wealth and prosperity. It can be placed in the home or a place of business to open the doors to abundance.

Grid: Seed of life

Master stone: Iron pyrite

Way stones: Citrine

Desire stones: Peridot

Affirmation: "The money I need comes to me quickly and easily."

When crafting your affirmation, you can change it to state the exact amount of money that you need, or name the specific job you want. You can also place folded money or a coin underneath your master stone.

Protection Crystal Grid

This protective grid can be made to shield yourself or your space from many different things. It can protect from spiritual or energetic forces being directed at you, or it can be programmed to protect against illness. It can even be designed to ward off a specific person. Black crystals are most commonly used in protection grids.

Grid: Hexagon

Master stone: Black tourmaline

Way stones: Obsidian

Desire stones: Onyx

Affirmation: "I am protected completely from (that which you need to guard against)."

You can place this grid near the entrance of your home. If its purpose is spiritual protection, keep it in your meditation area. Be sure to activate it every day with a wand to maintain its strength. Energy emanates outwards from this grid, so try not to have objects nearby that could interfere with it, such as other crystals or metals.

Success Grid

The spiral grid creates a pattern of increase and expansion, which is a perfect fit when it comes to success. Success is something that grows over time, like the spiral shape, building upon various experiences and achievements. This grid is to bring victory to your personal endeavors whether in business, health, or personal life.

Grid: Spiral

Master stone: Carnelian

Way stones: Citrine

Desire stones: Tiger's eye

Affirmation: "I am succeeding at (task)."

Place this grid wherever it is you pursue your goals, whether that's in your office, with your workout equipment, or near your art supplies.

Crystal Grid to Find Love

The stones in this simple grid create a combination of sexual attraction, emotional connection, and admiration. After making this grid, keep an open mind about who comes into your life; love sometimes happens in surprising ways.

Grid: Tripod of life

Master stone: Garnet

Way stones: Opal

Desire stones: Rhodochrosite

Affirmation: "I'm in a loving, supportive relationship with a wonderful person."

The tripod of life grid is perfect for initiating new beginnings, making it the best choice for grids to attract new love and relationships. Keep this grid in your bedroom, or near where you get yourself ready for dates or events where you're hoping to meet someone.

Grid to Manifest Psychic Ability

If you're a tarot card enthusiast or interested in developing your psychic abilities, create this grid in the area where you perform your readings or hone your divination skills. This grid is also useful for boosting your intuition.

Grid: Triangle

Master stone: Prehnite

Way stones: Selenite

Desire stones: Moldavite

Affirmation: "My psychic powers are strong and dependable."

Moldavite can be expensive, so a good substitution in this context is amethyst. You can keep a single crystal in your bag or box or tarot cards, or choose a gemstone pendulum based on its properties.

Grid for Confidence

Sometimes it seems like everywhere we look we see something to shake our confidence. This grid is designed to combat those detrimental outside influences and helps you focus on your strengths. The crystals in this grid all share strong, passionate energy. The sunstone brings self-esteem, the tiger's eye promotes courage, and carnelian can fire up your belief in yourself.

Grid: Spiral

Master stone: Sunstone

Way stones: Carnelian

Desire stones: Tiger's eye

Affirmation: "I am confident and secure, and I know my worth."

The spiral grid is useful in this context because of its ability to make a small thing replicate and grow bigger, causing self-confidence to build on itself over time.

Chapter 6: Further Information

Now that you've learned the basics of healing crystals and grids, there are a few further considerations going forward. This chapter covers some miscellaneous information that you'll find useful on your journey.

Crystal Interactions

Some crystals will be damaged by water, salt, or sunlight. Below is a list of these to look over while deciding which crystals to work with, and which methods you'll use for cleansing and charging. Remember that any crystal that can't be placed in water or salt for cleansing can be exposed to smoke or earth instead. For those that can't be charged with sunlight, try the full moon. Not all of the crystals listed below are included in chapter three, but you might encounter them in the future and can refer back to this list as needed.

Crystals that will be damaged by water:

- Aragonite
- Azurite
- Calcite
- Celestite
- Iron pyrite
- Fuchsite
- Labradorite
- Lapis lazuli
- Iccland spar

- Malachite
- Selenite
- Tourmaline
- Turquoise

Crystals that will be damaged by salt:

- Amber
- Azurite
- Calcite
- Lapis lazuli
- Malachite
- Moonstone
- Opal
- Selenite
- Topaz
- Turquoise

Crystals that can fade in sunlight:

- Amethyst
- Aquamarine
- Celestite
- Citrine
- Fluorite
- Kunzite
- Opal
- Sapphire
- Smoky quartz
- Topaz
- Turquoise

Advanced Crystal Grid Information

Starting out with crystal healing and gridding can be overwhelming, which is why this information was kept until the end of the book. After you've gotten accustomed to your crystals and how to use them, you can begin building upon your knowledge. Here is some further information to consider when selecting your own stones for gridding.

Crystal Energy Lattices

Each crystal and mineral has one of six internal lattice structures. A lattice structure is a microscopic pattern of geometric shapes that continuously repeat and expand infinitely. A crystal's ability to direct, hold, or intensify energy is impacted by its lattice structure. There are six categories of crystals based on this information: Seekers, enhancers, guardians, dispellers, barriers, and attractors.

Seekers

Seeker crystals have a hexagonal structure. Seeker crystals help guide you to what you need and want, opening the way to manifestation. Some seeker crystals are:

- Agate
- Amethyst
- Aquamarine
- Calcite
- Carnelian
- Chalcedony

- Citrine
- Emerald
- Jasper
- Onyx
- Quartz
- Rhodochrosite
- Tiger's eye
- Tourmaline
- Unakite

Enhancers

Enhancer crystals are formed in the isometric system. Their formation contains perfect cubic building blocks. Enhancers can improve what we already have, leading to enrichment of the self and our lives. Enhancer crystals include:

- Fluorite
- Iron pyrite
- Lapis lazuli
- Sodalite

Guardians

Guardians form in the monoclinic crystal system, made of parallelograms. Guardian crystals provide protection on the earthly and spiritual planes. They're included in grids to protect property, emotions, and energy. Common guardian crystals are:

- Chrysocolla
- Howlite
- Jade
- Malachite
- Selenite
- Serpentine

Dispellers

Dispeller crystals form in the orthorhombic system, which means their lattice is composed of diamond shapes. Their energy is directed outward and can banish illness, pain, and negativity. Some examples of dispeller crystals are:

- Aragonite
- Celestite
- Peridot
- Topaz

Barriers

Barrier crystals are formed in the triclinic system and contain trapeziums. They project energy in all directions and create a protective barrier on all sides. Barrier crystals are effective for shielding against illness and misfortune. Barrier crystals are:

- Amazonite
- Kyanite
- Labradorite
- Moonstone
- Rhodonite
- Sunstone
- Turquoise

Attractors

Attractors form in a tetragonal pattern. They help draw things into our lives. They work best paired with other crystals rather than alone.

- Rutile
- Zircon

Gridding a Large Space

Earlier on, you learned all about making small crystal grids that can fit on a table or other small surfaces. With that basic knowledge, you can now make grids that are the size of a room, an entire building, or a piece of property. All the same techniques apply, just on a larger scale.

Most rooms are a square or rectangle shape, so it's easiest to base your grid on squares. It's possible to use more complicated grids in a room, but it would require you to carefully measure and mark the space beforehand. That being said, there are area rugs on the market that feature sacred geometry.

To make a crystal that lays over your whole living room, you would put your master stone and affirmation in the center of the room, perhaps on a coffee table. From there, put your way stones around it in the shape of a square (you might have to ask other members of the household not to move them). Then, put your desired stones around the perimeter of the room. If you place them along the floorboards where they meet the wall, your desire stones can be concealed by furniture or decor. This is okay; they're still going to work. To activate a grid of this kind, stand near the center of the room with your wand. Walk around the room, tracing the pathways from the master stone to your way stones, and then from the way stones to your desire stones. You'll have to move around the room to do so. There's no need to move furniture to do this; you can point your wand towards the crystals and the energy will reach them regardless.

This same technique can be applied to gridding a building or a piece of land.

When gridding structures or property, it's helpful to include as many natural influences as possible. This allows your grid to flow with the existing magnetic forces of the earth. The main magnetic line runs from North to South. If you're using a grid with long straight paths, align them with the North and South poles with the help of a compass.

Another way to enhance your grid with nature is to build it in the path of the sun and the moon. To do this, begin your grid at sunrise or moonrise. Place a crystal in the exact direction that the sun or moon appears over the horizon. Throughout the day (or night), place your crystals on the ground in the direct path of the sun or moon above you. When the sun or moon sets, place your crystal in the direction where it goes down. Build the rest of your grid around this line. The solar and lunar path shifts throughout the year, so you'll need to adjust your grid accordingly.

Conclusion

Once your eyes have opened to the hidden world of sacred geometry and crystal healing, it changes the way you see the earth, the universe, and beyond. It shows us that we are made up of the same matter as the stars, the oceans, and the earth, revealing how everything is connected. It shows us our place in the big picture. Going forward, you're going to notice more and more evidence of our interconnectedness, especially when you put your crystal grids into practice.

By now you have the foundational knowledge to practice crystal healing in your own life. You can refer back to this book as a reference guide in the future as you deepen your knowledge and practice. When you're confident, try intuitively creating your own crystal grids and see what happens!

You've learned all about the physical healing properties of crystals, and how the mind, body, and spirit are all one. Often, physical pain is a result of the misalignment of our emotional and energy bodies. Crystal healing treats the spirit and mind in order to access the physical.

Maybe you have already started your own crystal collection and can identify some of the properties each one possesses. Keep in mind that how you feel about each stone matters just as much as what any book says. Everyone's energy field is slightly different, so just because someone else vibes with amethyst, doesn't mean you will. Be open to the experience and understand that it's an intensely personal one that goes beyond books and lists.

If you've tried cleansing and charging your crystals, you'll have witnessed for yourself the difference in energy before and after this process, which demonstrates again the interconnectedness of all things. Everything on the planet works together in a perfect cycle of giving and receiving.

When you try out different grids, you'll probably discover that you prefer some more than others, or that some seem to yield better results. Keep experimenting and remember to listen to your intuition. You have learned the basics and now it's time to bring the voice of your own spirit into the mix.

Being aware of the basic building blocks of the universe and realizing that you can harness that ancient power is a transformative realization. You'll see for yourself how these timeless laws of nature exist within and without you, in all you see and experience. This leads to transcendence and spiritual awakening, with a mind-blowing understanding of your place within the perfect universe.

As you tap into the power of crystals, you're engaging in the same mystical activity as ancient societies, calling upon the power of time and space. When you hold a crystal in your hand, you hold a piece of the cosmos, containing the passage of thousands, maybe millions of years. Care for your crystals as the sacred, incredible things they are. They will enrich your life, your health, and nourish your spirit for years to come.

References

Hall, J. (2009). The definitive guide to over 200 crystals. v. 1. Godsfield Press Ltd.

Heilbron, J. L. (2013). Platonic solid | mathematics. In Encyclopædia Britannica. https://www.britannica.com/science/Platonic-solid

Lindburg, S. (2020, August 24). What Are Chakras? Meaning, Location, and How to Unblock Them. Healthline. https://www.healthline.com/health/what-are-chakras#the-7-main-chakras

Mabelle, E. (2020). Crystals for Witches: Rituals, Spells, and Practices for Stone Spirit Magic.

Mason, H. M., & Petrofsky, B. (2016). Crystal grids : how to combine & focus crystal energies to enhance your life. Llewellyn Publications, Ltd.

Newman, T. (2017, September 6). Reiki: What is it and are there benefits? www.medicalnewstoday.com. https://www.medicalnewstoday.com/articles/308772#where-can-I-get-reiki

Ozaniec, N. (1994). Chakras for beginners. Headway, Hodder & Stoughton.

Tuan, L. (2017). CHAKRAS : the seven doors of energy. Lo Scarabeo.

University, G. S. (2019, December 3). How the Golden Ratio Manifests in Nature. Treehugger.

https://www.treehugger.com/how-golden-ratio-manifests-nature-4869736

www.ingramcontent.com/pod-product-compliance
Lightning Source LLC
Chambersburg PA
CBHW071213120626
46546CB00006B/2541